EXPLAINING
The truth about Christmas

DAVID PAWSON

ANCHOR RECORDINGS

This revised edition published in Great Britain in 2019 by
Anchor Recordings Ltd
Synegis House, 21 Crockhamwell Road,
Woodley, Reading RG5 3LE

**For more of David Pawson's teaching,
including DVDs and CDs, go to
www.davidpawson.com**

FOR FREE DOWNLOADS
www.davidpawson.org

**For further information,
email: info@davidpawsonministry.com**

ISBN 978-1-911173-77-9

This booklet is based on a talk. Originating as it does from the spoken word, its style will be found by many readers to be somewhat different from my usual written style. It is hoped that this will not detract from the substance of the biblical teaching found here.

As always, I ask the reader to compare everything I say or write with what is written in the Bible and, if at any point a conflict is found, always to rely upon the clear teaching of scripture.

David Pawson

1

I was asked to record some thoughts about Christmas and this first chapter is historical – where it all started and where it all came from. Then in the second chapter we will look at the Bible and the actual story of the birth of Christ and how all this fits together, or even whether it does fit together. As most people probably know, Christmas is not a Christian festival; it began long before Jesus Christ was born. It was originally a pagan fertility cult and it was a celebration of the winter solstice – the fact that the sun was just beginning to get stronger again. They waited until the solstice was over on December 21st and then celebrated the sun being born again, and that spring is on its way again.

Because of course people used to live much closer to nature than we do, and were much more dependent on the seasons. Their food didn't come and stay in the refrigerator or freezer all the year round, they had to depend on the seasons for their food. So this was a matter of celebration – especially during the cold, dark winter it was good to have a carnival, which is what it really was. Now it was mainly in Europe that this began, and in northern Europe it was the festival of Yule. That was the origin of the Yule log and Yuletide, for one of the central features of the celebration was a huge bonfire around which they kept warm. For that they used to chop down a big tree and burn the trunk as the Yule log.

In southern Europe it was called The Saturnalia after the god Saturn. The Romans celebrated Saturnalia and made a great deal of the sun god Mithras. So it was a celebration of nature. It was part of a fertility cult. Fertility then was a very important feature—fertility in the fields, fertility of the animals, and of the people. So there was this annual carnival or festival, which I am afraid developed into quite an indulgent festival because the normal rules of life were cancelled for the festival. It wasn't just one day; it was twelve days and lasted until January 6th.

Even today I remember in our home decorations had to be taken down on that date – the twelfth day. I had no idea why. I didn't then know about the twelve days of Christmas, when "my true love said to me...." Of course, that is a clue to what went on. Normal restraints were removed and all kinds of things happened as a result. For example, the normal rules of social relationships were cancelled. Therefore, one part of it was that there were no longer upper and lower classes over Christmas. They often changed places. Indeed, masters would serve servants their meals on that day. There is a survival of that in the British army. It is still the custom at Sandhurst for the officers to serve the privates Christmas lunch. It is a reversal of the social order just for a time.

But it was mainly in the realm of sexual relationships that the release came and restrictions were removed. That is still seen in office parties. Kissing under the mistletoe goes right back to these festivals when they decorated their homes with evergreen, like fir and holly, and above all, mistletoe. All these evergreens were taken in and used to decorate the home, and putting a wreath of holly on your front door goes right back to those pre-Christian festivals. One of the features was very amusing. In the carnival they could dress up how they liked, and they reversed the sex of people dressing up, so men dressed as women and women dressed as men. We have still got that today. In every pantomime the principal boy is a girl with the longest legs, and the mother of the principal boy is a "Dame", who is a man. That is a cross-dressing which goes right back to the carnivals of the original mid-winter festival.

There are more things than that I would like to mention. It was a time of gluttony, when it didn't matter how much you ate. You could eat yourself under the table, and that was alright at Christmas. That still happens with Christmas dinner, and the turkey and the plum pudding, when we eat far more than we normally eat for lunch – it is a relic of the old fertility festival. The drinking too: you could drink as much as you would like and drink yourself under the table. That, too, has survived. Again, at the office party or over Christmas the pubs are full of people getting drunk.

What else has survived? Well, the social rules are reversed, the sexual rules are reversed. The eating and drinking rules are set free and, interestingly enough, gambling, which was normally frowned on during the year – at Christmas you could really gamble as much as you liked. That certainly has a modern counterpart in the money that is spent over Christmas, which leaves many people in debt to face the New Year and pay off what they have had on credit over Christmas. So all these things go right back to those twelve days of Christmas. Many communities elected a lord of misrule, who ruled over the twelve days and had the freedom of any woman in the community during those twelve days. That is the origin of the twelve days of Christmas, "when my true love said to me...."

So we have a very indulgent festival when people simply let go and could do what they wanted. It was a self-indulgent festival. But there was a good side, and it was that the rich were expected to help the poor over Christmas. The haves were concerned about the have-nots, and especially the poor, the lonely and the disabled were a special concern. That was a good feature of the annual winter festival, and it has survived. Boxing Day is when the boxes in church were emptied for the poor and the boxes were then used to distribute whatever had been put into them on Christmas Day, to those who were needy on Boxing Day.

Well, that is how it began. It went an up and down sort of journey through the ages. I will just mention one or two of the downs and one or two of the ups. During the Middle Ages it wasn't particularly popular except among the aristocracy and the upper classes. Then it steadily declined over the centuries until the nineteenth century, and then Christmas as we know it really began, when two authors wrote stories about Christmas. On this side of the Atlantic, it was Charles Dickens. Much of what we know of Christmas today we owe to him. Not just his book *A Christmas Story* and Scrooge. As to the turkey in that story – the turkeys came over from the States originally and there was an author called Washington Irving, and he was the Charles Dickens of America. So the modern Christmas developed on both sides of the Atlantic in a kind of cross-fertilisation and set off by these two authors – their stories really raised interest. But I suppose the biggest factor over this side of the pond was Queen Victoria and her husband, Prince Albert, from Germany. Our kings had a strong German taste about them, and they had already brought Christmas over.

Some of our kings and queens were very keen on the celebration, the carnival aspect, the buffoonery aspect; Henry VIII celebrated and Elizabeth I was known to dance and gamble on Christmas Day. Right through the Stuart and the Tudor times, Christmas was celebrated particularly by the royal family. But it was Victoria and Albert who focused on the family as the main celebrating unit – not the community but the family; they stamped family life on Britain. It was Albert who introduced the Christmas tree to Britain. Germany being full of forests, he introduced the Christmas tree to the home as the main visible sign of Christmas. During Victoria's reign it became a major part – every family had to have a Christmas tree.

During the nineteenth century someone thought of sending a Christmas card to your relatives and friends. A card was relatively simple and cheap. The penny post became the halfpenny post for Christmas cards. That difference between letter and card postage lasted quite a long time, right into the twentieth century. So this was a quick and easy way of greeting your relatives or friends. Instead of writing long letters, all you would do was sign a card and send it off for a halfpenny.

So it is to the nineteenth century that we really owe the modern Christmas – in particular, a gentleman who is known on this side of the Atlantic as Father Christmas, but on the other side of the Atlantic as Santa Claus. That name came from Holland, because New York, in which Santa Claus had first appeared, was a Dutch colony called "New Amsterdam". In Holland there was a strong emphasis on a saint from long ago called Saint Nicholas, a bishop from Turkey who was a very kind man, concerned for the poor. There was in Turkey a father who had three daughters who had no chance of getting married, though they were good looking, because they didn't have any money for a dowry, and a bride or her father was supposed to supply money (the dowry) and the peasant couldn't. So good Saint Nicholas smuggled some gold coins wrapped in a cloth into the cottage of the peasant. He didn't climb down the chimney and he didn't put it in a stocking, but he wrapped these gold coins in a cloth and threw them through the window, and the three girls were able to get married. Now this story really captured the Dutch imagination and Saint Nicholas became almost their patron saint. They called him Sinterklaas, which is short for Saint Nicholas. Then, in New

York, Santa Claus as we know him was born, and given red robes edged in white ermine, and with hunting boots and a long white beard. We had the Santa Claus that we know.

I remember when we had our little three children in Buckinghamshire we took them out in the car one morning to go and see Santa Claus in a big shop. But on the way we saw another Santa Claus getting on a bus, and we saw yet a third Santa Claus walking along the street. I remember the confusion this led to with our three children. Santa Claus seemed to be everywhere we went that morning. Of course, he is everywhere now, he is part of Christmas.

So, all that happened in the nineteenth century. I will tell you in a moment about the Christians who opposed it all quite strongly. But public sentiment was too strong for the protestors. What has been added in the twentieth century to all this? Well, there is no question about it: the biggest thing is commercialism. In October there are already the advertisements for Christmas displayed on television and the shops begin to stock up for Christmas, and so on.

It is interesting that the bulk of the advertising is aimed at children – very expensive toys, too. The twentieth century Christmas focus on children is something which the Victorians did not do. Children could be seen but not heard then, but now children have become the focus of Christmas for many families.

Another thing that has been added is what we call the Christmas Broadcast of the Queen. It has become a ritual, and you can't imagine Christmas without it now. But it was begun by her grandfather, George V. He made the first Christmas broadcast and quoted that memorable thing: "I said to the man who stood at the Gate of the Year...." The reply of the man was, "Put your hand into the Hand of God and you can go into the future safely yet." It really struck a chord in the nation when King George V quoted that, and therefore he went on making a radio broadcast every year. But his son, King George VI, stopped it because of his dreadful stammer. You may have heard of the film *The King's Speech* and know all about that stammer. In the first year of World War II, for the sake of the soldiers who were away from home, he was persuaded to make it. He managed to do it and he kept it up, right through the war. So his daughter, our Queen, has to make the Queen's Royal Broadcast and it is part of Christmas now, as is television entertainment.

It is interesting that all the mass media now cash in on Christmas. As early as, I think, 1900, *The Times* never mentioned Christmas in its December issues. But if you look at newspapers and magazines today, Christmas takes over for a time and becomes the main subject.

So those are the historical features, none of which are Christian of course, and all of which have so gripped the public sentiment that the thought of abolishing all that would really horrify the public.

One other twentieth century addition to the mess is Rudolph the Red Nosed Reindeer with his shiny nose – that has become now such an important part of Christmas. So it is a funny mix.

Well now, let me just begin to look at how Christians have coped with this annual pagan fertility custom. In the first four centuries, good Christians ignored it. They really were convinced that Christians should not be involved in such an indulgent thing, and the carnival aspect particularly worried them. In the fourth century, Pope Gregory sent a missionary to England called Augustine – not the Augustine who wrote the *Confessions*, the other one. There was one in Africa, the one we know best, but another Augustine was sent to England and he reported back a year or two later he had made progress – he had baptized the King of Kent; he had a number of people coming to a church, which later became Canterbury Cathedral. But he said, "I have not been able to wean the British off their annual fertility cult festival," namely Christmas, though it wasn't called that then. Try his best though he could, he could not get them off this indulgent activity. So he asked Pope Gregory, "What can I do about it?"

Pope Gregory virtually said, "If you can't beat them, join them." But what he actually said was, "Baptize it into Christ; bring it into the Church and do it in the name of Christ." Furthermore, he suggested, "As they celebrate the birth of the sun, you can say, 'We'll celebrate the Sun of Righteousness,'" who has risen with healing in his wings. That is a quote from the Old Testament.

So December 25th became the official birthday of Jesus. Of course it isn't anything of the kind – he wasn't born in December. Shepherds don't watch their flocks by night in December, there is often snow on the hills of Israel then. We are told in the Bible when he really was born, which was not anything like December. But just as the Queen has her own birthday, and an official birthday when they have the parading of the colour at Horse Guards Parade, so now Christ was given an official birthday, which was not his birthday but was celebrated as such. That was the profound beginning of a Christian Christmas.

What was included to make it especially Christian was a Roman Catholic Mass. Then the name "Christ-mass" came into being, and it has been known as that ever since. So this was the Roman Catholic Church's missionary strategy. If you couldn't get people to drop things, then bring them in and make them part of the Church's programme and that will keep everybody happy. I am not convinced about it at all.

But in the Philippines and in Latin America I found that Catholics still practise animism and spiritism because that was their original religion and the Catholic Church encouraged it to come in. It is quite disturbing to find out how far these old things are still deeply rooted. So that was the beginning, and it was Pope Julius, following Pope Gregory, who made it an official institution of the whole Church, though it was originally only for Britain and to get the British to drop certain things.

Over the medieval period there was a steady decline of interest, but there is still a medieval feel about Christmas — stagecoaches on Christmas cards and old thatched roofs, you have seen them all. There is a kind of nostalgia for the good old days. They weren't all that good, but nostalgia looks at them through rose-coloured spectacles. Now all that changed radically when the Protestant Reformation came, as we shall see in the next chapter.

2

We have seen that by the medieval period Christmas had become an official Christian institution and the church gave its full support. Significantly, much of the pagan practice of Christmas continued. Even as late as the fourteenth century they were still electing lords of misrule to reign over the twelve days, so that we have a period during which the pagan customs and the Christian approval were moulded together and continued side by side. With the Protestant Reformation, mainly Luther and Calvin, there came a big change. Luther struggled with anything Roman Catholic, and of course, Christmas was a Roman Catholic creation. He also struggled with the pagan roots of Christmas.

Nevertheless, Martin Luther gave in, as most state churches did, because when you are a state church you regard yourself as including everybody. You pastor a country, and therefore the tendency in state churches is to keep public customs and sentiments. So Luther did celebrate Christmas, reluctantly, but especially he loved his guitar and singing songs and carols to the children. So he kept it.

Calvin, on the other hand, in Geneva did the opposite. Calvin strongly opposed Christmas and Easter because the New Testament is opposed to festivals of any kind. So Calvin, in Geneva, would not have anything to do with Christmas. Calvinism in the form of Presbyterianism came to this country

– but to Scotland, not so much to England. The result is Scotland has no Christmas. They celebrate Hogmanay, or the New Year, but they don't celebrate Christmas. Presbyterians don't, they follow Calvin. John Knox was Calvin's man in Scotland and he persuaded the Scots to drop Christmas altogether, as in a later time when the Presbyterians nearly took over England as well as Scotland in the civil war.

When Cromwell came to power and the Royal Family was abolished and King Charles lost his head in a crisis, then what happened was that legally Parliament in Britain abolished Christmas altogether. Of course you can't abolish popular sentiment as easily as that, and in the country areas particularly they kept up some celebration of Christmas. But officially it was now abolished in England as well as Scotland. However, you know the civil war led to a Republican Britain with Cromwell as the First Protectorate, or head of it all. It only lasted a few years and the people wanted a king again. They wanted Charles II back on the throne, and they got him back on the throne and he reintroduced all the Royal Family's support of such carnival activity. Christmas was back on the agenda.

In the nineteenth century, as mentioned earlier, the Christmas as we know it really came to be, with the trees and the decorations. Gradually, these things crept into the church towards the end of the nineteenth century, until in the twentieth it was quite common for a church to have a Christmas tree right in the place of worship. I was amazed a few Christmases ago to find a Pentecostal church in which the church had a huge Christmas tree and the church itself was decorated with Christmas streamers and so on. So, gradually, the churches capitulated to the popular desire to go on celebrating Christmas.

Indeed, the churches began to cash in on it themselves. For example, they replaced the service on Christmas morning with Holy Communion on Christmas Eve, and found they got more taking bread and wine on a Christmas Eve than at any other time during the year. Even Evangelical churches today can put on a Christmas Eve communion. Churches put on carol services and sang carols instead of hymns.

So, gradually, churches gave in, and what has been called "the cult of the crib" began. This was that churches should have a model crib with the baby Jesus in it, and Joseph and Mary and donkeys, and sometimes camels, and all sorts of creatures. They used to make a display of the crib and make it a place of devotion and veneration. From there, the cult of the crib spread into society and the nativity play was born – especially when children were expected to act out the story of the birth of Christ, leading to some very amusing situations. When you are trying to make little children act like adults you can expect trouble. I think of one nativity play in a primary school where the three kings came on and the first one said, "Here's some gold for the baby Jesus," the second one said, "Here's some myrrh for the baby Jesus," and the third one said, "And Frank sent this" – and presented the third gift to the baby Jesus.

I recall another nativity play where Mary and Joseph, Mary being great with cushion, arrived at the inn and said, "Is there room at the inn?"

Little Joseph said, "You can see my wife is nearly ready to give birth to a child, we need a room."

The boy playing the landlord had forgotten his lines and said, "Come on in! You can have the best room in the house for Mary!" The whole thing was getting off course.

Fortunately, the boy playing Joseph had great presence of mind, and he pushed his head in through the door and came back and said to Mary, "You should see the state of this inn; it's not fit for you. We'll be better off in the stable, come on," and turned the whole play round again, to the great delight of the parents watching.

The Christmas story is not for children, it is an adult

story. The Bible was written for adult believers. Anyway, that is how Christians came to be involved and this has led up to another crisis. In America you had the churches deeply divided over Santa Claus and Christmas. On the one hand, the Presbyterians, again from Calvin, and the Baptists and the Quakers, together raised a howl of protest against churches accepting Christmas. It is often from those quarters that we still have a protest.

The mainline denominations tended to bring Christmas in. The Free Churches at first tended to keep it out, but most of them, Methodist, Congregationalists, gave way. I have to say Baptists, Salvation Army, and even Pentecostals have given way and usually celebrate Christmas in some way or another, which raises the whole question of, "Where are Christians today and what should be their attitude?" We have a choice before us: either to take it in and try and keep it somehow well-behaved or to reject it and not even try.

Or, to put the situation quite bluntly, either we can try and put Christ back in Christmas or we can take him out of Christmas and let it go its own way as a pagan festival again. Britain is increasingly secularised and the second most godless society on earth (Japan being the first according to a poll of the nations) – that is not saying "not religious", just godless. So we are up against a changing situation, that if it goes on as it is, the trend is entirely towards a secular Christmas that has more in common with the pagan origin than with anything specifically Christian.

I have to be honest with you, I am in the second group, and I don't observe Christmas and I don't preach it. I talk about it but I believe the safer way is to free Christ from all that has come up around Christmas. I will tell you why I have come to that conclusion. It is a bit startling. But at the Pentecostal church which was in Croydon where I preached at Christmas time, though I was horrified to see all the tree and the decorations right inside the church, I did a thing that I have often done and asked the Lord questions. I call it "interrogatory prayer." I hope you practise that. You have heard of intercessory prayer, where you pray for other people. But interrogatory prayer is when you ask the Lord questions and wait for an answer. I have found that a very helpful form of prayer, but a very startling one when the answer comes. In the middle of the service I said, "Lord, what do you feel about Christmas?" He reminded me that I had a photograph album at home, which was produced by my mother who was a very keen amateur photographer, and she used to win competitions. This album is of me and my life, from a little baby right through to a boy.

When I show it to people they say, "Oh, what a lovely baby," and I hate it. I want to say, "I'm not a baby! You have to relate to me now as I am now, not as I was then!" Much easier to relate to a baby – they don't answer back. You can coo over them and you pick them up and cuddle them, but they don't fight you (not usually, anyway). So there was this album and I had it at home. I thought, "Why should the Lord remind me of that?" Then I realised that he wanted to say to the people: "I'm not a baby, not now. You have to relate to me as I am now, or it is not a real relationship."

I realised that cooing over a crib is not a real relationship because it is not with a real person, it is with a doll. If you want to be related to Jesus now you have to relate to him as he is, a full-grown man with his character what it is. When all the world is so excited about a little crib with a doll in it, Jesus is saying, "I'm not like that now. I want a relationship with you that is real between you and me as I really am." I shared that with the congregation because it came to me as I sat there on the platform.

The other thing that has had a big influence on my thinking was that years ago I met with some leading Christians in this country and we decided to engage in interrogatory prayer to find out more about our Lord. Together we said, "Lord, we'd love to know you better, would you please share with us some of your own feelings?" We then made it quite specific; "Is there anything that makes you feel sick," which is an unusual question. I'll never forget the moment, my blood runs cold almost. Suddenly, for more than one person in that circle who were praying, just came one word: "Christmas". I think from that moment I began to have serious thoughts about it. Now there is nothing wrong with a family festival, nothing wrong with family reunions – nothing wrong with having a happy time together, and if that is the way you want to celebrate the cold dark winter, do so. Don't make Jesus the excuse for it. That is my plea. Don't think that he is excited about it. How important it is for Christians not to think, "What do the churches say or do," but, "What does Christ himself think or feel about it?" Try asking him and see if he gives you the same answer he gave us on that occasion. But find out what his real thoughts are.

Do you know that far fewer people are converted at Christmas than at any other time of the year? That is because most evangelists are not busy over Christmas. They are home with their families and they find they can't get appointments over Christmas to hold a crusade, so they seize the opportunity to have a bit of family life. There are fewer people – there are more people taking bread and wine at midnight communion, but far fewer coming to Christ. He has a very raw deal out of it all. I just leave that thought with you because every Christian today must, I think, face up to the fact of Christmas. We can't get away from it, it's all around us and we have to decide what we are going to do about it.

Well now, on the back of all that, let's go back to the Christian story of Christmas and look at it afresh. It's much more than in a school nativity play. So I want to begin now to look at the biblical Christmas, and you find it in the Gospels. The story is an amazing mixture of natural and supernatural, and how seriously you take the supernatural part will have a big effect on how you celebrate Christmas.

The natural part is really quite ordinary. There was nothing very different about the birth of Jesus. After some hours of labour, and in not very nice circumstances, Mary brought forth her firstborn boy. That birth was quite normal. It was not a miraculous birth.

It wasn't in a stable – that is part of the myth. It wasn't in a cave, though if you go to Bethlehem today they will show you a cave in the crypt of the big cathedral there, which they believe to be the cave where Jesus was born. They also show you a spot on the floor of the cave marked with a silver cross where Mary's milk was spilt. It is quite objectionable, the whole thing. He was born in an inn, but not in a room in the inn. There was no room in the inn, but he was still born in the inn. Because if you go to a middle eastern inn, even today you have a big square wall with no windows in it surrounding the inn, pierced by two big gates or a big double gate at one side. When you go in, you see rooms all around the inner side of the wall and all the windows face inwards, and in the middle is a space with troughs for water and mangers for food for the animals. All this is for security and safety in a dangerous world. You take your animals and family into the gates and then you ask, "Is there a room for us?" The clear biblical record is there wasn't a room available, which meant that they had to do what others had to do, and that is camp in the courtyard in the middle, where the only place to put a baby was one of the troughs. That is the picture. So Jesus was born under the stars in the open air in the courtyard of the inn. Do you see the picture now? Most Christmas cards have got it altogether wrong—either a stable or a cave or something. There is no word "stable" in your Bible. He was born where the animals and his family were spending the night.

Photo above is an example of a modern day Inn.

It is a very ordinary story of taxes, poll taxes, and a pregnant fiancé of a young man. He was probably about seventeen or eighteen and she would be fifteen, which was the normal age for betrothal in those days. There they are. Why are they so far from home? The answer is she was pregnant before marriage, and that was in those days, as it still is in many circles, a disgraceful event. She would be boycotted in her home town of Nazareth, nobody would help her. They wouldn't talk to her; they would just leave her alone. So she had to give birth somewhere else. Since Joseph, her fiancé, had to go to Bethlehem for the poll tax because he belonged by his ancestry to that town, she had to go with him. A seventy-mile journey on a donkey is not a thing that a woman advanced in pregnancy would normally undertake, but she went.

Now it is amazing how many myths and legends have grown up around this birth. We had shepherds who came to see her – well there is nothing mythical about that. But then came "wise men". It simply says "wise men". But legend has said they were kings. The origin of that whole thing is that they brought three gifts, and therefore it was thought there must have been three of them and they must have been royal. Who else would come to a King? And they have been given the names. Well, all that is just not true. It is fiction. So you have this strange mixture of fact and fiction.

All the fiction isn't included. Many of Jesus' own cousins were assassinated because he was born in Bethlehem. King Herod was jealous, and he ordered the killing of every baby under two years to make sure that this baby born to be king of the Jews would not survive. When did you last see that on a Christmas card? The soldiers of Herod slaughtering the babies—there must have been dozens of them, and most would be related to Jesus because the people who had come to Bethlehem to be taxed were all of the same extended family. Did you ever hear that preached about at Christmas? It is all part of the true story, but we select from the story what we like and we then add to it anything that improves the story in our imagination.

Oh, we even sing about it. Did you ever sing *Away in a Manger* and about the baby that never cried? "No crying he makes"—rubbish! The only way a baby can let its mother know that he is hungry is by crying, and to think that Jesus was so holy that he never cried – that is a ridiculous idea. But we have sung it heartily, or at least got our children to sing it. Whenever you see the picture of Jesus' birth you see golden halos over the baby. It is a symbol of glory, but it was never seen by anyone.

I have a real admiration for Joseph. Named after the Joseph of the Old Testament, he was a dreamer as well, and he got messages from God in dreams. The first message he got was when he discovered that Mary was pregnant. He was horrified and he even thought he would have to break off the intended marriage and have a proper divorce from his fiancé, because betrothal was serious then.

Well, Joseph believed the dream when God told him, "I'm the Father" For the first time in history – such a thing, fancy Joseph believing it! Yet he believed it, and the very next morning he married Mary to cover up even admitting or acknowledging that the baby was his, at great personal cost. I love Joseph. He doesn't say much in the story, but he does an awful lot in response to dreams.

3

Let us look at the facts of our Lord's birth. The first fact is he was not born in December. He was born somewhere around the end of September or the beginning of October, for the seventh month of the Jewish calendar bridges our September and October. It was during that time that the Feast of Tabernacles was held. It is quite clear from the Bible that Jesus was born in the Feast of Tabernacles. How do we arrive at that? With a very simple bit of mathematics—nine plus six, which is fifteen. With that simple sum you now know when Jesus was born. We're told that his cousin John was born to Zechariah and Elizabeth. When Zechariah went into the temple and was told that his wife, who was way past childbearing, would have a son and be called John that was how John the Baptist began.

Now when the angel Gabriel came to Mary and told her that she would have a son even though she had never known a man, he also said, "And the proof will be that your cousin Elizabeth is also, amazingly, pregnant at her age." Immediately, Mary set off to visit her cousin who lived in a little village near Jerusalem. When she went into the room, her cousin Elizabeth felt the baby inside her jump – the first time she felt that. She said, "My baby jumped for joy when you came into the room," and they shared what had happened.

Now it says that was when Elizabeth was six months old or six months gone. Nine months later, Jesus was born. Six plus nine is fifteen. If we knew when Zechariah went into the temple and was told he was going to have a son and add fifteen months to it, we'd know when Jesus was born. Do you follow me? Well, from the Second Book of Chronicles, we know in chapter twenty-four there is a list of the priests who had a rota to go and serve in the temple. Zechariah's turn to serve is listed there. He was the eighth out of twenty-four.

Therefore, a third of the way through the year Zechariah went into the temple. When you add the fifteen to that, you come to the seventh month of the following year, which is the Feast of Tabernacles. Every Jew believes the Messiah will come at the Feast of Tabernacles. It is written in their scriptures; it is written in their culture. So that is when they expected him. You find in the Gospel of John that the Word of God became flesh and "tabernacled" among us. You also find out that Jesus' own brothers who were sceptical of who he was, when the Feast of Tabernacles came around later in John's Gospel, said, "It's the Feast of Tabernacles, you'd better go and show yourself in Jerusalem if you're the Messiah." They were teasing him. They knew that the Feast of Tabernacles is when he should come.

I am also convinced that is when he will come again. I can't tell you the year, but I can tell you the month. It will be in the seventh month, and that is when Jews all over Israel celebrate the future coming of the Messiah, and they have that in that month precisely for that reason. So he was born end of September, beginning of October. The biggest miracle in Jesus' birth was not the birth itself, though that is where the world focuses when they celebrate Christmas. The real miracle happened nine months earlier; it was his conception that was supernatural because Mary had never had a sexual relationship with a man.

Now that is not the only virgin birth there has been. A professor of gynaecology in London University once told me that there have been probably six or seven, virgin

26

births in the human race recorded or claimed. But he said the one thing that convinced him the claims were possibly established was that in every single case the result was a baby girl. It would have to be a baby girl. The scientific process is called "parthenogenesis", when a female egg spontaneously divides and produces an individual without having been fertilised. It is common in the vegetable world. It is not unknown in the animal world; the Komodo dragon is one species that has virgin births. As I have mentioned, there are records of it happening to humans, but never to produce a boy. So here undoubtedly is an amazing miracle.

We now know enough about conception and birth to know what could have happened, and there are three possible things that God could have done in Mary's womb. First, he could have created a complete initial foetus and planted that in Mary's womb. If that is what happened, then God was the Father, but Mary would not have been the mother. She would not have contributed to the foetus; she would be a surrogate mother, nothing more than an incubator. So it can't be that.

The second thing that could have happened: The only difference between a male and a female foetus is in one tiny chromosome and in every cell in my body every chromosome looks like a letter y; in my wife's body, that chromosome looks like the letter x. All that God needed to do was just a tiny bit of genetic modification to use the term that is popular today. Now if that were the case, Mary would have been the mother, but God would hardly have been the Father.

The third possibility, the one I incline to, though I wouldn't be dogmatic on this, is that God created a male sperm bearing the DNA of divinity and fertilised one of Mary's eggs with his created sperm. That would mean that Mary was fully the mother and God was fully the Father and the resulting child would be human and divine together. So it is that third possibility that appeals to me.

However, the miracle is that Mary produced a baby boy without the help of a man. That has never been heard of before or since. Let us go a little further. I have told you that I think Joseph must have been a fine young man to believe in a dream and act upon it. In a second dream he was warned about Herod and took Mary and the baby as refugees to Egypt, where no doubt they had to sell the gold, frankincense, and myrrh just to keep alive. Then, later, when Herod died they came back to Nazareth. So he only had two dreams. We don't have a single word that he ever said, but he acted on those two dreams. To believe on them and act on them must have taken tremendous faith. I am looking forward to meeting Joseph.

Now Mary. Protestants say far too little about Mary. Again, the Roman Catholics have said far too much, and we have reacted against that and we say far too little. I have heard so many sermons about other characters like Peter and Paul and John, but rarely heard a sermon about Mary – but she was the first charismatic. She was the first one to say, "Whatever the Holy Spirit wants to do with me, I'm willing," and she spoke in tongues on the day of Pentecost. I have never heard all that mentioned, have you? But it is there in your Bible. Mary was a most wonderful woman.

I enjoy preaching on Mary, and I have done so in front of a bunch of sixty Roman Catholic priests with a cardinal sitting in the middle of the front row. My subject was what the Bible really says about Mary. I said it doesn't say anything about her Immaculate Conception or her Perpetual Virginity—she had more children, at least seven of them after Jesus—or about her bodily assumption to heaven. I went through the four dogmas that the Roman Catholics believe, and I said that none of them are in the Bible. But I said, "You have discouraged us from preaching what is in the Bible about Mary because you have added so many things that aren't in the Bible" – one of which, a very important one, we will come back to.

Now as a human being Jesus had a beginning. But when you write the story of Jesus, where do you begin? Mark began with his baptism because that's when his public ministry began. Matthew went further back and began with his birth, tracing his family history back to Abraham. Luke went further back than Abraham. He went back to Adam because Adam was the ancestor of Jesus.

Finally along came John and he went back to the very beginning. He took the words from Genesis 1 – In the beginning, he already was. That word "was" is very significant. Not in the beginning he began, but in the beginning he was already there. Since the human mind can't go back beyond the beginning of all things, you just can't imagine when there was nothing, not even space. John is saying: at the very beginning he already was there and he was face to face with God and he was God. Of course the Jehovah's Witnesses have had to change that in their Bibles; they don't accept Jesus' full divinity.

But this means that Jesus' birth was unique – not in the way he was born, but in the fact that he chose to be born. Nobody else in the whole of history has ever chosen to be born as a baby. You didn't, I didn't; you didn't choose your parents and I didn't choose mine. We had no choice, but Jesus had, and he chose his parent and chose to be their baby. That is the most amazing thing, and yet I have never heard it mentioned in any nativity play. Did you? I never saw it on a Christmas card. I would love to see a Christmas card saying: "The man who chose to be born." Now there is a truth for adults, not children. It makes you think.

The problem that John had was: if he existed before his birth, even before his conception, what was he called? He only got the name Jesus after his birth and he only got the title "Christ" when he became the Jewish Messiah, that is what it means. He only got the name "Lord" after his resurrection and ascension. So what was our Lord Jesus Christ called? John, with his inspiration of the Spirit, called him "the Logos" – that is the Greek for "word", but it is much more than word.

John was writing his gospel in Ephesus where there was a man called Heraclitus who was the father of modern science. He taught his students to use their eyes to observe what went on and to find out the reason why things happened as they did. The word for "reason why" is "logos", and every branch of science has the word "logos" in it; psychology, physiology, zoology, meteorology. Every one is a study of how things behave in that field – until you know the reason why. So meteorology studies the weather and asks why the clouds come and drop rain or why the wind goes a particular way. That is the basis of all science, and John called Jesus "the Logos" because he is the reason why everything else behaves as it does. Isn't that a lovely title?

So in the beginning was the Word, the Logos, the "-ology" of our research and all our questions. He is the reason why. He is the answer. Then he wrote these amazing words: "The Word, the Logos became flesh and tabernacled among us" – pitched his tent among us, lived among us. That word "flesh" is very important. I want to add five adjectives to bring across the sheer wonder of it. The Word, the logos, the reason why the second person of the Godhead – who had always existed along with his Father, but chose to become a baby – took upon himself physical flesh. You could touch it. He could touch people, they could touch him. It was real physical flesh such as you and I have.

Secondly, it was male flesh, not female. I know Jesus has been claimed to be both male and female. The most famous picture of him, knocking at the door was by Holman Hunt who used three females as models for it – one for the long ginger hair, one for the face, and one for the figure. It is a thoroughly female Jesus in that picture, so I am not too fond of it. Jesus was male. He came to show us God, and God is a Father, not a mother. He is King of the universe, not the queen. He is husband of Israel, not the wife. Therefore, to show us God the Father it had to be male flesh, whether we like it or not.

Thirdly, it was Jewish flesh. He was born and circumcised as a Jew and is still Jewish, yet most Sunday school pictures of him are of a Scandinavian with fair hair and blue eyes. That is not Jesus. He was Jewish with a Jewish nose and he's still Jewish and always will be. The next thing is that it was sexual flesh. There has been a kind of common impression that Jesus was sexless. If that is so, then he didn't have the problems that I have and that every male has and he didn't overcome them as he calls us to. It was sexual flesh, and in his teen years particularly he must have had sexual temptations.

There was a film that caused an outcry called *The Last Temptation of Christ*, directed by Martin Scorsese. It imagined that Jesus had sexual temptations. Well, that is true. He must have done. It was male, sexual flesh. But he didn't give way to any of the temptations that brought, he overcame them.

Finally, and this may be a shock to you, the New Testament says his flesh was sinful flesh. Now we rebel against that. We think, "No, he was without sin." Yes, he didn't sin. But he was made in the likeness of sinful flesh, which means he took on our human nature and had that battle to face as we have to face. If it wasn't sinful flesh then he hasn't fought our battles and can't give us the strength to. But he has been tempted in all points, like as we are. The three points we are tempted in are the world, the flesh, and the devil, and Jesus was tempted in all points just as we are. Now that is a truth that many Christians can't accept.

The Catholics have invented the Immaculate Conception of Mary to get around the problem, and they believe that Mary was born without sex or without sexual temptations, and therefore she was able to produce a boy that didn't have sinful flesh. But if Jesus was born of Mary then our nature was passed to him through Mary and he had the battles we have, but he never gave in and he won the battle. It's Paul who says, "He was born in the likeness of sinful flesh," Romans 8. People say, "Ah, just a moment. He says he was born in the 'likeness' of sinful flesh, you mean just the appearance." No, the word "likeness" means exact reproduction. It's used in Philippians 2 where it says he took on himself the likeness of human flesh. That really means he was reproduced as human flesh, and Paul says the same thing of sinful flesh.

I finish with this very direct question: do you think it is appropriate to mix this pure Son of God with all that goes on at Christmas? With the office party? With the mistletoe? With all the rest of it? With the huge expense? With all the money that is spent, even on the children? Do you think it is fitting to put Christ in the middle of that? The one thing that is certain is nobody is going to be able to abolish the sentiments of Christmas that come from its pagan origin. There have been so many attempts to clean up Christmas through the centuries, that when you read the history of it you realise it never succeeded. These things should not have been brought into the church, they should have been left outside. People coming to Christ should be told: leave these things behind; don't bring them in with you.

So we are left with that basic question: do we want to mix Christ up with all that? And I am afraid that my answer is: no we don't. Let us rescue Christ from Christmas. Let us celebrate his birth when it really happened. It is much cheaper and simpler to do so. Let us separate Christ from all that is not of him and let us worship him as he ought to be worshipped. That is my final word on Christmas.

ABOUT DAVID PAWSON

A speaker and author with uncompromising faithfulness to the Holy Scriptures, David brings clarity and a message of urgency to Christians to uncover hidden treasures in God's Word.

Born in England in 1930, David began his career with a degree in Agriculture from Durham University. When God intervened and called him to become a Minister, he completed an MA in Theology at Cambridge University and served as a Chaplain in the Royal Air Force for three years. He moved on to pastor several churches, including the Millmead Centre in Guildford, which became a model for many UK church leaders. In 1979, the Lord led him into an international ministry. His current itinerant ministry is predominantly to church leaders. David and his wife Enid currently reside in the county of Hampshire in the UK.

Over the years, he has written a large number of books, booklets, and daily reading notes. His extensive and very accessible overviews of the books of the Bible have been published and recorded in *Unlocking the Bible*. Millions of copies of his teachings have been distributed in more than 120 countries, providing a solid biblical foundation.

He is reputed to be the "most influential Western preacher in China" through the broadcast of his best-selling *Unlocking the Bible* series into every Chinese province by Good TV. In the UK, David's teachings are often broadcast on Revelation TV.

Countless believers worldwide have also benefited from his generous decision in 2011 to make available his extensive audio video teaching library free of charge at www.davidpawson.org and we have recently uploaded all of David's video to a dedicated channel on www.youtube.com

TAKE A LOOK AT YOUTUBE
www.youtube.com/user/DavidPawsonMinistry

THE EXPLAINING SERIES
BIBLICAL TRUTHS SIMPLY EXPLAINED

If you have been blessed reading this book, there are more available in the series. Please register to download more booklets for free by visiting **www.explainingbiblicaltruth.global**

Other booklets in the *Explaining* series will include:
The Amazing Story of Jesus
The Resurrection: *The Heart of Christianity*
Studying the Bible
Being Anointed and Filled with the Holy Spirit
New Testament Baptism
How to study a book of the Bible: Jude
The Key Steps to Becoming a Christian
What the Bible says about Money
What the Bible says about Work
Grace – *Undeserved Favour, Irresistible Force
or Unconditional Forgiveness?*
Eternally secure? – *What the Bible says about being saved*
De-Greecing the Church – The impact of Greek thinking
on Christian beliefs
Three texts often taken out of context:
Expounding the truth and exposing error
The Trinity
The Truth about Christmas

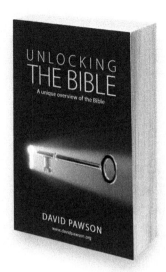

UNLOCKING THE BIBLE

A unique overview of both the Old and New Testaments, from internationally acclaimed evangelical speaker and author David Pawson. *Unlocking the Bible* opens up the Word of God in a fresh and powerful way. Avoiding the small detail of verse by verse studies, it sets out the epic story of God and his people in Israel. The culture, historical background and people are introduced and the teaching applied to the modern world. Eight volumes have been brought into one compact and easy to use guide to cover both the Old and New Testaments in one massive omnibus edition. *The Old Testament: The Maker's Instructions* (The five books of law); *A Land and A Kingdom* (Joshua, Judges, Ruth, 1&2 Samuel, 1&2 Kings); *Poems of Worship and Wisdom* (Psalms, Song of Solomon, Proverbs, Ecclesiastes, Job); *Decline and Fall of an Empire* (Isaiah, Jeremiah and other prophets); *The Struggle to Survive* (Chronicles and prophets of exile); *The New Testament: The Hinge of History* (Mathew, Mark, Luke, John and Acts); *The Thirteenth Apostle* (Paul and his letters); *Through Suffering to Glory* (Hebrews, the letters of James, Peter and Jude, the Book of Revelation). Already an international bestseller.

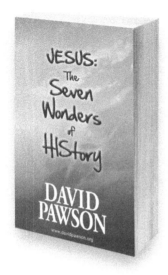

JESUS:
THE SEVEN
WONDERS
OF HISTORY

This book is the result of a lifetime of telling 'the greatest story ever told' around the world. David re-told it to many hundreds of young people in Kansas City, USA, who heard it with uninhibited enthusiasm, 'tweeting' on the internet about 'this cute old English gentleman' even while he was speaking.

Taking the middle section of the Apostles' Creed as a framework, David explains the fundamental facts about Jesus on which the Christian faith is based in a fresh and stimulating way. Both old and new Christians will benefit from this 'back to basics' call and find themselves falling in love with their Lord all over again.

OTHER TEACHINGS
BY DAVID PAWSON

For the most up to date list of David's Books
go to: **www.davidpawsonbooks.com**

To purchase David's Teachings
go to: **www.davidpawson.com**

Lightning Source UK Ltd.
Milton Keynes UK
UKHW020744090922
408600UK00009B/796